NARRATING AUDIBLE BOOKS AT HOME
A STEP-BY-STEP GUIDE

RACHEL EDWARDS

For those wishing to audibly read, tell, and express their own stories. Consider this your invitation to a literary "show and tell."

EPIGRAPH

Tell me a story out of your mouth
So I can fall asleep
With words performed on closed-eyed sets
My cast and future told for me to keep.

— RACHEL EDWARDS

CONTENTS

Introduction   ix

Prologue   1
Chapter 1   3
Unlocking Your Inner Narrator
Chapter 2   6
Stepping Into Audible
Chapter 3   9
Managing Your Audible Project
Chapter 4   13
Setting The Stage And Equipment
Chapter 5   15
Mastering Bringing Text To Life
Chapter 6   18
Revealing the Techniques
Chapter 7   21
Creating, Uploading, and Processing
Chapter 8   23
Breaking It Down: The Basics of Audiobook Economics
Chapter 9   25
Holding Our Breaths
Chapter 10   28
Choosing DIY For RLE
Epilogue   32

INTRODUCTION

TELLING STORIES OUT OF MY MOUTH

As night skies settled around our country farmhouse in Virginia, my mother would start the difficult task of getting me to sleep each evening. The routine was predictable and the bedtime stories read from chapter books with female authors: Laura Ingalls Wilder, Astrid Lindgren, and others. Female narrators shaped my dreams and imagination. When the evening chapters were complete, I would beg my mother to tell me "stories out of her mouth" until sleep finally drew me through the darkness softened by a mere nightlight. A notoriously poor sleeper, those stories were always my favorite and offered by maternal figures and voices. Usually, they were stories created about my life or theirs...and I could visualize every character. Hearing the tales and phrases of memorable family or community members mingled with imagining them interacting with book or television actors.

My appetite for storytelling and make believe was enormous. I entertained myself by playing with imaginary plots gleaned from television shows and books I learned to read far earlier than expected.

As a voracious reader, I never lost my love of escaping within pages and word descriptions. I wrote countless expositions and character sketches into blank notebooks with carefully selected writing instruments.

Self-publishing first beckoned during elementary school at Unionville Elementary School in Orange County, Virginia. I was the type of student who loved school, teachers, and anyone with precious school supplies. As the daughter of a teacher and administrator the mere smell of a public school represented a feeling of home- the earthiness of pencil leads and sharpener shavings, the lemony chemicals buffing the floors, the blending of household smells twisting morning optimism and evening recess through children's and faculty days.

Second grade was the first self-production of binding books with heavy card stock, paste, and wallpaper sample pages. That year resulted in two books: *The Day I Got My Ears Pierced* and *All About School*. The entire process captivated me and continues to this day. Often my objective is to preserve memories for family or share words in neatly bound books. *Audible* and podcasts empower and preserve my own voice for others- family, friends, or strangers who feel like both.

The early reading experiences continued with a love of classroom read alouds in all forms and eventual revivals in my own teaching career. Long before audiobooks slipped into popular culture, I loved reading aloud and clung to literacy experts who touted the beneficial practice for students of all ages.

The most unusual thing I have professionally accomplished is to produce books for the audiobook giant, *Audible*. At least that is what I have surmised by the twinkle of interest in the eyes of those who ask what I am doing following a career of teaching high school and middle school English. People seem genuinely curious. The questions about getting started or confessions of dreams of authorship accompany the "lean" and "tilt" of their heads and torsos…and I have stumbled over my explanations more than once. More than anything else, I love glimpses into the dreams and ambitions of others. *Narrating Audible Books At Home: A Step-By-Step Guide* allows me to share the process.

INTRODUCTION

Through ten collaborations and five independent projects, I learned our experiences shape our expectations. Each step of self-publishing touched an earlier life lesson, created knowledge, and revealed storytelling memories. If I enjoy working at my own pace and meeting my own writing objectives, maybe other authors could also benefit?

If I could figure out how to produce my own *Audible* books at home, would others want that same option? After learning through collaborations with other authors, I tested my methods with my own publications and found the same results. I liked the process and found it empowering...which feels like an authentic experience worth sharing.

As I tell you the steps I use to narrate my own *Audible* books at home, brief examples will help describe my journey and offer a layout designed to meet platform approval.

PROLOGUE

I don't remember the exact wording of the *TikTok* video that shifted my entire life. The confident social media influencer seemed to have an idea too good to be true. My memory may paraphrase the content as I needed to hear it. "Can you read aloud and record yourself? If you want to make money reading books, sign up as a narrator with *ACX.com*." Work with authors, read books, and narrate? See manuscripts before publication and be part of a writer's vision? A dream career combining all of the things I loved? Yes, please.

Despite having no idea what I was really signing up to do, my enthusiasm outweighed my professional audiobook experience. I found *ACX.com* online and completed my profile as a narrator. The only narration experiences I could list were about loving reading and middle schoolers asking me to read another chapter aloud. I certainly didn't have documented accolades or memberships in professional groups. The website provided directions for a vocal sample and my technical trial-and-error journey launched.

I had no idea *ACX.com* was *Audible and iTunes.*

I researched what was needed to complete my profile as a narrator and found a phone app for recording MP3's. The technical parts were what most concerned me- this was vastly different from *Google Class-*

room or simply connecting a microphone and speakers to my computer.

Needing a piece to read for my sample, I located a favorite poem a neighbor wrote for my aunt. I recorded and submitted the raw audio to complete a narrator account. I will never understand why Jessica Roe selected me to read *Nothing Like Him* based on my sample. I didn't know any of the audio requirements or responsibilities of a narrator, yet. But I always read with passion, emotion, and respect for an author's work. Hopefully, that's what she noted in the inspirational poem.

I narrate the way I read and hear a piece in my head. With the same reading voice I have experienced books since my earliest memories, I embrace words. Years of reading aloud to my students and my son shaped my focus. I was immediately fascinated by the entire publishing and production process.

My recording and editing methods are simple, basic, and do it yourself. The steps are organized around the questions I ask myself and provide a framework for audiobook development. If I can produce my own books, so can you.

Allow my prologue to be yours.

CHAPTER 1

UNLOCKING YOUR INNER NARRATOR

Will an audience want to hear my Audible?

Does this also sound like you? You independently published a book. The kind of book that makes you want to read, escape from reality, and enjoy an interesting cover. A personal memoir detailing words you need to detach, move forward, and grow into your best new chapter? A work of fiction that you always dreamed of writing and know you must narrate? An author within an exploding self-publishing new frontier.

Social media, fans, and book reviewers tell you about the magnitude of your work. Your literary and personal voice are described as engaging, authentic, and confident.

Family members, friends, and colleagues are on the fence about your writing. Should you have a more recognizable publisher to be considered a writer? Others cheer with enthusiasm. You simply love the journey and are happy to disprove critics.

Should I narrate and produce my own book?

You believe in yourself and potential to change the literary landscape. At least you think you do, self-publishing may feel difficult to master or explain to others. Sometimes, the entire process feels a little lonely and disconcerting.

Self-doubt can creep in along with the highs and lows of problem solving and getting your book in hand. With so many changes happening in the various platforms and on social media, it's hard to keep up and feel knowledgeable.

Especially creating the audiobook versions for folks who claim not to read, fans who beg for your voice, not to even mention the stories you are secretly holding, unwritten... how are you supposed to make *that* happen? Successful authors and scholars should just *know*, right? Storytellers... just *must* be born that way.

But you can't imagine anyone else reading your story aloud.

Choices, my friends, you have choices. Down & Dirty (basically, do it yourself) at home or a GAT3 in Charlotte, NC (a marvelous professional studio with top of the line recording equipment and sound engineering)...your book, your stories, your voice, your choice. You can hire narrators or share royalties. You can assemble teams to help assemble your audiobook or outsource the entire project to a company. Production budgets range from less than $100 to several thousands.

I *am* "Down & Dirty" and a "Do It Yourself-er"...and that phrase tends to mean stories or experiences I am not sure if I am supposed to talk about or admit experiencing. Do my production methods take away from my work?

Narrating my own writing is never a question in my mind. I am comfortable reading to others and recording. How to publish paperbacks and ebooks were far bigger hurdles as a new author. Does it matter if I really don't have ambitious goals of every book becoming a best seller? The whole process excites me and takes me right back to second grade. So, for me, I choose to work backwards from where I have the most experience and feel the greatest audience interest- *Audible*.

I often hear authors say they just don't know where to start. I didn't know, either. I would have devoured a resource answering questions I didn't expect to encounter first narrating and later writing. *Narrating Audible Books At Home: A Step-By-Step Guide* is organized by my personal process and what has led to successful productions.

If you want to narrate and produce your own book, do it. Or, at least, try…you won't be disappointed by your learning experience. From any frustration will come growth and a uniquely created audiobook.

We can do it together.

CHAPTER 2

STEPPING INTO AUDIBLE

*W*here do I start producing my own Audible?

The hardest part may be knowing where to start. If you want to create an *Audible* for a book you have self-published, go directly to the *ACX.com* platform. Select "Authors Who Narrate" and complete the entire account profile. All of it. After all, you are living with stories, content, and a voice that wants to be heard. Once you have completed your account and made decisions about royalties, more questions will follow about producing your title. Take your time and remember you are the decision maker.

What should I have completed before finding and claiming my book title on ACX.com?

Since *ACX*, *Kindle Direct Publishing*, *Kindle*, and *Amazon* are all part of the *Amazon* family, books published on those platforms will transfer information with relative ease. If you have worked with other companies, you may need to directly communicate with *ACX* for approval to create and add your audiobook.

Titles should be available through *Amazon* in paperback form. Otherwise, you will not be able to claim and initially start the development process.

Will my cover art meet ACX's expectations?

ACX will provide specifics for audio expectations and cover art. *Getcovers.com* has become my current favorite website for developing covers for paperback, ebook, and *ACX.com*. When I place my initial order, I also request my audiobook cover not contain important information in the lower right corner. Covers are a significant amount of my "Do It Yourself" budget. I embrace services that eliminate technology challenges and frustration.

Why do I continue to choose Audible for my audiobook productions?

Since I *accidentally Audible-ed,* I received some hard lessons when I didn't know all the industry terms. Not every audiobook is an *Audible*...just like not every tissue is a *Kleenex*. *ACX.com* is the development/production website for *Audible* and *iTunes*. Audiobook production companies vary in title selections, narration requirements, distribution, and price.

Audible's familiar name, insistence on human voices, and production options outweigh concerns about such a large platform and fine print. Navigating their website's backend requires self-sufficiency, perseverance, and wading through Frequently Asked Questions sections. I find the process thrilling and often overlook minor frustrations with the *Amazon* grouping of companies. Rather than pay others to complete services, I would rather work within the giant corporation's features and benefits.

After setting up a completed account on *ACX.com*, even the most confident authors have a tendency to feel overwhelmed by the production process. By reviewing obstacles holding back your voice, identify, comprehend, and eliminate those barriers to develop your audiobook.

Despite the website having most answers available, the initial barrage of decisions may feel overwhelming. Use the *ACX* website to reclaim your power and confidence. Print the requirements for royalties and production of a completed audiobook. Whether you are choosing to involve other parties (audio engineers, studios, narrators) or produce yourself, these resources are significant for a positive experience. It's simply a good idea to be aware of options for future publications. Awareness of possible expenses and potential savings by completing tasks yourself, may also provide some extra motivation.

This is the application and practice I use for creating my own audiobooks. This method is designed by (and for) someone who feels personal satisfaction accomplishing "Do It Yourself" projects.

When working with any technology and online platforms, some variations and personal problem-solving should be expected. Every effort has been made to minimize variations between my experiences with the *ACX* platform and audiences intending to create their own audiobooks. There will always be new technology and platforms in the competitive world of publishing. Some changes are welcomed and others frustrating; however, deep breaths and patience are always helpful parts of our personal toolboxes.

CHAPTER 3

MANAGING YOUR AUDIBLE PROJECT

Am I qualified to narrate my own books?
That's a conversation an author must have with themselves. By *ACX's* standards, most likely, you will be able to meet their expectations and fulfill your own sound goals. Professional training is available; however, I didn't initially opt for that after so many years of reading aloud. My writing style tends to align with my straight forward performance- and I find narration cathartic. I love producing my own work and creating my own timelines.

The 2022-2023 growth statistics for *Audible* and countless other articles support the continued expansion of self-publishing and the audio industry. Some genres naturally nudge authors toward self-narration and an eager *Audible* community of consumers.

Record a few sample chapters and share with others for feedback. I found my friends and family were excellent critics of my vocal delivery, recording area, and background echoes. I learned how personal listening experiences are for everyone and incorporated many of their suggestions.

If the technical components of recording and audio engineering produce overwhelming anxiety, connect with a professional studio and work with them to create your audiobook files according to *ACX* requirements.

How much time do I need to produce my Audible?

Production time will vary for each author and project. I multiply each anticipated finished hour of audio by three. Generally, by taking *ACX's* initial suggestion of narration length per project and tripling, I can create a reasonable recording timeline. Make certain to note as soon as you have claimed your title, files may begin being uploaded. Finished projects are typically available within ten business days of final submission to website. With that being said, set deadlines for production.

Treat yourself with some extra care as you determine your first personal deadlines. Be flexible and extend your marketing budgeting by saving a "Now Available On All Platforms" campaign until your audiobook joins its ebook, paperback, and hardback companions.

Am I ready to narrate?

The fine print decisions of your *ACX* account may require some introspection and forward thinking. Once you consider who will want to access your audiobook and your overall objective to reach your audience, the fine print (royalties, distribution, book categories, and descriptions) should feel livable...at least for your current project.

Before you start producing your audio files for *ACX.com*, make sure the book manuscript (and copyright) is accessible and able to be added to your account for audiobook development.

The website will offer search options to import book details from *Kindle* and *Amazon*. Remember, they are all part of the same production "family" and the uploading/publishing experiences will often mirror. I start with *Kindle Direct Publishing* and work through adding ebook, paperback, and finally audiobook.

Audiobooks are not intended to include the exact layout as your paperback or ebook. Accomplish this initial content import and preview audiobook expectations/requirements. Save yourself any frustration or surprises during future uploads of audio files. For example, audiobooks on *Audible* currently do not allow sections about the author- an expected standard in paperbacks-and that imported section title will be eliminated and content ruled unnecessary in final upload. So, preserve your time and voice by creating a narration plan correlating requirements for finished audiobook. I plan my entire manuscript *around Audible.* If a section will not transfer between paperback and audiobook, chances are, I evaluate and include in another way.

No matter where you plan to publish your files or record audio for release, check the fine print for expectations, requirements, and distribution copyrights/royalty.

Naturally, authors already know how they expect a chapter to sound; however, literal readings and voice projections, may only allow a few chapter recordings a day. Each chapter and section will be recorded in separate files.

As an *Audible* "Author Who Narrates," give yourself grace to learn obstacles that may hinder your project timelines- most of them will depend on your personal schedule, recording environment, and vocal preferences.

Believe it or not, simply pressing record may cause some nerves and awareness of vocal intonations and word pronunciations not anticipated. Add some additional time to first project outline to account for multiple takes and minimize stressful recordings. As you become more comfortable with your narration process, your confidence will grow and production times more accurate.

As an author and narrator, choose practices that create the most positive experiences.

Even though I am not trained as a professional narrator, I learned a lot in educational trenches over the years. Mainly, I picked up what holds my interests as an audience member and reader.

My formal degrees, licensure, and anecdotes include:

Orange County High School Class of 1995.

This small town delivered a love of learning and stories. High school theater productions, elementary writing assignments, and the best in-class readings.

Emory & Henry College Class of 1999. Bachelors of Art in English Literature and Education.

Small college experiences with life-long impact. Fitting in for the first time with storytelling, big dreams, and writing.

University of Mary Washington Class of 2009. Masters of Educational Leadership.

Training to be a school administrator and embrace the whole child in an educational setting. Seeing the story behind textbook learning.

Licensed Virginia English Teacher and Administrator 2022-2032.

Engaging classroom reading, instructional design, and emphasis on dyslexia support through audiobooks. Eighteen years as an English teacher and thousands of incredibly memorable scholars.

Never underestimate the power of literacy and authentic voices.

CHAPTER 4

SETTING THE STAGE AND EQUIPMENT

What do I need to start recording?

I didn't intend to develop an inexpensive method for narrating and recording audiobooks. Honestly, I probably would have paid for expensive microphones and audio engineers given a longer deadline or formal training in narration. But my first collaboration for *Audible* felt like such a dream come true, I wasn't about to miss any check-ins or technical marks- my main focus was on reading the story with an engaging voice and meeting the author's vision for her audiobook. My first equipment purchases were combinations of familiarity from classroom read alouds and *Google's* suggestions to desperate software queries.

Voice Record 7 (Full) was my initial technology app to record a MP3 to complete my ACX profile. The program worked well with my *iPhone and Apple AirPods*. At that time, I was rehearsing recording myself and trying to find a good location at home without an echo or disruption. *Voice Record 7* had multiple features that matched the terms and numbers I was seeing from *ACX* and the ability to share with my honest support system of friends and family for feedback.

I invested in a home printer, updated *AirPods,* audio editing *Wave-Pad, Voice Record 7 (Full)* and noise cancelling foam pads. I "shopped my space" for office supplies, used my *Hewlett-Packard* laptop, and *iPhone*. When familiarity found technical success, I continued the process.

The first few collaborations had production times of about a month and I was all-in...every time, no matter what. I loved it. Romance books and fascinating characters were exactly what I needed in my life.

Where's my recording studio?

I determined a comfortable spot to record chapters and file sections. You must be able to eliminate voice echoes, outside noises, and potential interruptions to your reading. You will also need insulated wall space to post printed chapter pages for narration.

I use a corner of an interior bedroom closet and multiple closed doors. The surrounding clothes, blanket wall covering (clothes pins hot-glued, painters' tape connected, printed pages posted per chapter), battery-operated camping lights, and fleece curtain cloak works well for me. Simply put, find what works to allow best reading experience.

I sit directly on the carpeted floor and tuck my dog, Scout, into a tiny dog bed behind me. It took several productions for me to learn which items in my space caused extra noises or disruptions. My recording studio works for me and offers creative solace.

What equipment will I need for narrating at home?

Recording Devices- *Apple iPhone, Apple AirPods, Voice Record 7 Pro.*

Voice Record 7 Pro Settings- Advanced, MP3, Sample Rate- 44,100, Bit Rate-192, Bit Depth-32 , Channel-Mono, Encode Quality-High

Computer- *Hewlett Packard* for *Google Drive, WavePad,* audio files, and *ACX* uploads.

Once you have set your stage and gathered your equipment (or similar products and programs), take time to practice and share with others. Familiarity will only help as you press record.

CHAPTER 5

MASTERING BRINGING TEXT TO LIFE

What should I expect when reading my own work aloud?
Mistakes and fresh eyes are two anticipated variables. No matter how many times I proofread, I still rework after multiple print readings. When I narrate my own pieces, emotions prompt some altered expressions and require freedom for authenticity- if I am anxious about saying single words verbatim, my performance suffers. (When I know I need a professional studio and sound engineer for robust emotional release, I book one. But that's not exactly "Do It Yourself"- just another narration option I mention for authors.)

Most likely, your audience will not be comparing your audiobook and print versions for word-for-word accuracy. As a reader, I generally purchase one version of a piece of work- not paperback and *Audible*- unless there is a specific need or love. While narrating my work, sometimes, spoken word versions feel more authentic reflections of my writing intentions. I may even catch mistakes or adjust a word or phrase order after the sixth or seventh reading.

If I prefer my narration word choices and believe paperback version should be updated, I will revise my printed manuscript through *Kindle Direct Publishing.* Often, I have learned to read my own work aloud during revisions and editing final manuscript copies.

The cathartic release of reading my own work aloud and refining print version is a variable that breathes life into the text.

How should I prepare and rehearse?

After claiming my title through *ACX* to produce my audiobook, I print a physical copy of my book manuscript. Any portions of printed manuscript not meeting required audiobook outline are eliminated. Next, I separate each chapter into plastic sleeves and add to a three-ring binder. My annotation process is tedious and requires four or five readings per chapter- armed with my favorite highlighters, pens, and pencils.

Naturally, authors already know how they expect a chapter to sound, especially after completing the writing process. Literal readings and voice projections may only allow a few chapter recordings a day. As an *Audible* Author Who Narrates, give yourself some grace to learn obstacles that may hinder your project timelines- most of them will depend on your personal schedule, recording environment, and vocal preferences.

As I narrate my own work for *Audible,* the printed, silent, and spoken words will closely align and have similar sounds when read.

There may be some variations with punctuation or text features- because those features exist to communicate an author's intention and meaning to an audience. Be on the lookout for features that will need support: footnotes, graphs, captions, charts, abbreviations, etc. So, the practices may merge when the author is also the reader and know what they *meant* to write.

Remember when you first started writing and were told to put aside a rough draft to reread with fresh eyes later? Or to then read your writing aloud to catch mistakes? Generally, it is the same concept. This will benefit your ability to read with authenticity. You are now a vocal guide leading your audience through your work.

We tend to be our own worst critics. The first few narration sessions always provide some "stage fright" and anxiety. Once I have developed a recording and editing routine, my confidence returns. Pressing the record button should not be underestimated.

Microphones may pick up sounds you didn't even know your mouth produces with spoken words. No matter how many times you have read your book aloud in book stores, audio equipment and listening to playbacks, may cause some stress. The first few times through the process will allow you to hear the background noises eliminated through editing and sound quality improve.

Our reading experiences and annotation objectives are far more personal than one may expect. Since you do not want to spend hours analyzing every literal breath taken while recording, or editing out pauses that only distract you, find a meaningful method for marking reading notes for narration.

Does my audiobook need to be perfect?

No, but strive for almost perfect, interesting and engaging for an audience. Personally, I love an author's voice reading their work and wouldn't expect them to invest more in their *Audible* than their paperback version. My book production expectations closely follow what I want as a reader.

How much editing of audio files will I need?

I print each chapter, make narration notes, preview reading lengths, rehearse, and post within recording area for literal reading. That familiarity and repetition also encourages one-take-audio-capture and reduces editing needs. I strive to record each chapter with minimal detectable errors.

The repeated readings will also allow needed emotions to assist storytelling- or detach, and let the author voice and narrator voice play different roles.

As an author and narrator, choose practices that bring you the most positive experiences. Most, if not all, mistakes can be corrected between manuscript versions. This allows narration with greater confidence and vocal fidelity.

CHAPTER 6

REVEALING THE TECHNIQUES

*D*o production secrets exist?

Maybe, but most of my *"down & dirty"* strategies are part of a process that has met my production goals. Trial and error has made way for a "Do It Yourself" method that offers a framework or blueprint for authors. Accessibility for authors who want to self-produce *Audibles* often feels more like hard work, determination, and commitment- not a secret sauce.

What's the rehearsal game plan?

What types of chapters or sections are being annotated and prepared for narration? Generally, three chapters are reviewed and rehearsed for each recording session. Emotional or extremely detailed sections may reduce the number of pages for planned recording.

I make notes and highlight paper manuscript copies that remind me of all my childhood and classroom reading experiences. I read through and try to "hear" and notate each sentence. Are there pauses or vocal deliveries I may want to implement? Audio audiences will not be able to see italicized words or page layouts that contribute to understanding on a printed page. My voice will need to guide and communicate with intention any text features. Stumbling or mumbling through phrases will require repeated recordings or returned *Audibles*. More than that sobering thought of negative reviews, who wants to have a miserable experience narrating one's own written thoughts?

After annotations are complete and I start feeling the excited pull of the narration closet, pages are laid out and joined with painter's tape to post. The proximity of pages mean my eyes will not be forced to jump over white space to provide a cohesive read. I control as many variables as I can and opt for printed pages over digital. I then post my annotated and taped pages in my recording closet with clothes pins. Multiple chapter pages may be layered and then deconstructed after successful narration and transfer.

Once comfortably seated in my recording closet (which does strongly resemble a childhood blanket fort), I adjust my battery-operated camping lights and rehearse any chapter portions needed for vocal warm-up. I use battery-operated lighting and no-tech manuscripts to avoid adding additional background noises from electricity or swiping between screens. The main goal is to allow the vocal sounds to be recorded in best raw file format.

The loftier goal and game plan is to successfully narrate each chapter with vocal authenticity, engagement, and no detectable mistakes.

How do I actually narrate and record?

Recording Devices- *Apple iPhone, Apple AirPods, Voice Record 7 Pro.*

Voice Record 7 Pro Settings- Advanced, MP3, Sample Rate- 44,100, Bit Rate-192, Bit Depth-32 , Channel-Mono, Encode Quality-High

Computer- *Hewlett Packard* for *Google Drive, WavePad,* audio files, and *ACX* uploads.

Remember, record each chapter or section individually. Each chapter must have its own file.

Voice Record 7 Pro Application- Count silently five seconds at beginning and end of each chapter. Read work the way I want someone to experience it. When each chapter ends, I check playback option to make sure audio recorded, change the file title to be recognizable, and upload to *Google Drive*. Later, retrieve and download to laptop for editing and storage.

Google Drive- Download MP3 audio files to laptop.

WavePad- Open desired chapter file downloaded to laptop. (File/Open File)

-Listen to start of the selected raw chapter file. For our purposes, *raw* means unedited and unfinished recording of narrated chapters.

- Adjust/Edit/Effects- Select option to remove background noises. Scan and remove Brief Popping Noises. Next, scan and remove Background Traffic Noises.

-Normalize with- 27.650, -11db, peak loudness RMS, preset- simple peak, 3db headroom.

-Save with- Bitrate CBR 192, Mono, High Quality (wait until entire scan is finished to actually save).

After finished files are saved, test each completed chapter with *ACX*'s Audio Lab program under Production Resources on their website. This program can be accessed before audiobook submission and applies the same quality control software encountered during final upload. By using the Audio Lab programming throughout the recording process, authors can self-monitor and actively troubleshoot.

CHAPTER 7

CREATING, UPLOADING, AND PROCESSING

hat do I do after narrating all my chapters?

After recording and editing chapters and sections outlined in audiobook project outline, return to *ACX*'s website to prepare for uploading completed title. Review required final layout expectations: opening and closing credits, retail preview, and allowed introductory sections. *Audibles* are designed for best listening experience for consumers. Any manuscript portion not anticipated to meet that need is clearly eliminated by *ACX* parameters and will fail approval for *Audible* platform.

Select, narrate, and record required sections in their individual files. Commercial previews are incredibly important and give all audiences a chance to hear your voice before purchasing an audiobook. Make sure to select a sample that is engaging and encourages downloading.

Now that everything is recorded and checked by Audio Lab, what's next?

It's time to submit completed audiobook files. *ACX*, let's make these files into an *Audible*.

From your *ACX* account, select to add your completed audiobook. Even with the original book's Table of Contents beckoning on the screen, consult the *ACX* requirements. If uploaded files do not meet their requests, the audiobook will be returned for corrections.

Take a deep breath and calmly start transferring individual audio files. As each file loads, *ACX* programs scan for initial compliance. (This is why I use their Audio Lab to monitor my own finished files throughout the recording journey.)

If any audio files fail during the upload process, retrieve the raw audio chapter and complete needed adjustments. Keep all files until finished *Audible* is available on their app (*Voice Record 7 Pro*, unedited files, and finished files).

Once finished adding audio files, double check Table of Contents- remove category names that will fail approval, create desired chapter titles, and confirm files match each section.

Upload cover art that matches *ACX* requirements.

Finally, submit completed audiobook for review.

What happens next?

Reward yourself with something...anything...because receiving ACX's congratulatory email and notice quality control reviewers now have your voice within their checking software...may not quite satisfy your sense of accomplishment. In fact, it is a unique feeling that is difficult to describe to others. Excitement, pride, and a lot of nerves about production process. If all goes as expected, from the comfort of home an *Audible* has been produced.

But first, there are three to ten business days to wonder about those *Quality Control Gods* reviewing your hard work.

CHAPTER 8

BREAKING IT DOWN: THE BASICS OF AUDIOBOOK ECONOMICS

hat's the production cost for my audiobook?
(These are my out-of-pocket production costs.) Additional expenditures beyond the self-publication of the title, are kept low by doing it yourself. My *ACX* cover tile was part of my original cover packet completed with *GetCovers* and cost about $10. Printing my manuscript for annotating and posting for narration runs about the same as my *HP Smart* membership. Office supplies are reused for each narration and replaced when depleted (highlighters, pens, tape, and batteries). Operational expenses are included in household budget (Internet, cell phone plan, etc). Technology purchases and updates were made in an initial investment and reused (*WavePad $100, Vellum $249, MacBook, Voice Record 7 Pro, iPhone, AirPods*).

There is no initial charge to publish through *ACX.com* and I agree to their royalty terms. Since I am not extending funds to publish my audiobook and am doing my own narration, receiving 40% of each download does not seem unreasonable. Allowing *Audible* exclusive distribution also allows a significant number of promotional codes for free copies.

What if I had paid another narrator, split royalties, or worked with outside audio engineers, or studio? I would need to also monitor sales until my initial investment was recouped for my audiobook production.

Audible and ACX handle audience subscriptions, platform challenges, and continue to be the most robust and recognizable catalog in the audiobook world. Explore and monitor the *ACX* dashboard and personal profile to access promo codes, track sales, downloads, and royalty payments.

The cover I designed with *GetCovers* for *Narrating Audible Books At Home: A Step-by-Step Guide* includes significant personal images from my life. The frosty background is a picture my mother took one wintry morning in Virginia of my childhood yard. The coin is from my 2023 divorce settlement. Releasing my voice through narration allowed me to overcome a sense of *Audible Frost*. Often there is more than economic value or savings through adding your personal voice to your work.

CHAPTER 9

HOLDING OUR BREATHS

*W*hat happens if there's a problem with my submitted audiobook?

The first few uploads are the hardest- as with any new experience- and I completely admit initially feeling unprepared. I felt responsible for delivering a perfect audiobook as a narrator. *ACX.com* considers narrators as the producers of their audiobooks. For sake of clarity, it makes more sense to imagine narrators and authors collaborating on productions. I understand why many narrators hire audio engineers and charge per finished hour of narration. I was thrilled to be involved and was actively learning in the trenches of romance books. I was eager to please my authors and greatly respected their work. I learned many nuances of the *ACX* platform and *Audible* through these collaborations.

I also needed to meet ACX's requirements and learned from early quality control rejections. So, even if you think you have followed all of the fine print requests and requirements, sometimes, a submitted audiobook is challenged.

The requirements for audiobook approval are the same for Narrators and Authors Who Narrate.

Something needs to be changed and resubmitted for *ACX* to

approve your audiobook for *Audible*. Occasionally, despite best efforts, an email will arrive returning your audiobook for corrections. The first few audiobook projects and learning the platform's expectations are the most likely times for missteps.

Even though you may feel frustrated and confused, carefully read the entire email and determine the actionable steps needed for execution. Don't take it as a personal affront to your character or voice.

What if I reframe, personify, and give character traits to technology and self-publishing life to feel more connected to the practice?

Quality Control Gods are just using more intense software to match files to standards- with the number of *Audible* books currently on the market, I highly doubt they are "listening" to all our hours of reading. Make the needed adjustments from your *raw* audio files or cover art measurements and resubmit for review. If you attempt to adjust finished audio files, your overall sound will shift- not a great sound, at all.

Technology sometimes just *is awkward*.

Audible Frost (a phrase similar to imposter syndrome I use to describe vocal freezes from anxiety) ends with a pinging email alert.

What happens after I resubmit my audiobook after making corrections?

Publication and availability of your *ACX* audiobook through *Audible* and *iTunes*, arrives with a simple email notice. An author's hard work will magically be accessible for preview, purchase, download, and distribution.

You will also receive a second email notice announcing access to your free downloads to distribute. Surprise! Typically, in my experience, each title receives about fifty...but, some platform variations may change over time.

Still, I always love this feature. Explore the *ACX* dashboard and your profile to access promo codes, track sales, downloads, and royalty payments. As you copy and paste codes to family and friends, remember to slide the toggle bar to keep track of the shares.

Whether that happens on business day four or ten, the feeling of accomplishment must come from within *you*. Is it a big deal? Absolutely. But, maybe, the world won't immediately recognize how much work you put into receiving that notice of acceptance.

Congratulations! Celebrate.

Just as you did with your first printed or published work, design a plan to share your voice with others. Direct all the traffic you want to your new audiobook- new ways are developing all the time.

Without downloading your book, previews allow your storytelling voice to be heard- that's also why selecting that section is so important for audiobook design. First impressions tend to *sell* a book. Direct sharing from within the *Audible* app to text messages may be an appealing way to encourage those who are technologically hesitant.

Who will receive your announcements? Fun instructions for how to listen, learn, and experience your work?

Finding new ways to share your voice and stories are all part of the excitement.

Prices for *Audible* subscriptions, downloads, and royalties will continue to wiggle as the market continues to grow. Frequently check the app itself for new features, hiccups, and marketing ideas. You may also notice some royalty payment differences between platform families (*Kindle Direct Publishing, Amazon, ACX, Kindle, etc.*)

If you are already in the self-publishing worlds, you already realize new digital babies and programs are birthed almost daily.

More than anything else, take some time to celebrate your voice. If everyone knew how to produce their own *Audibles*, I doubt there would be so many companies charging big money to do it for you.

There is really nothing like the first time you hear your own voice on *Audible*. Since the platform is so popular, remember to connect your *Alexa*, share through iPhone, social media, and email.

Exhale, you made it.

CHAPTER 10

CHOOSING DIY FOR RLE

*W*hy do I DIY?

Do It Yourself for Rachel Lyn Edwards. I have come to embrace the entire process of self-production and narration. Feeling projects come together during times of inspiration and creativity offers immense satisfaction.

Growing up with a large extended family of educators, learning and research have always been part of my day-to-day life. Producing resources, documenting family history, and finding stories within pictures are passed down just like my resemblance to my beloved mother.

Transferring handwritten stories, letters, and pictures into print, allows me to make sure future generations can access family stories in their own learning styles. By printing and publishing word-for-word from original texts, an author's voice is heard through their punctuation and word choices. Narrating those pieces allows me to feel incredibly close to the writers.

Who inspires the DIY?

My inability to rest until book projects are complete has a lot to do with proving things to myself. When working independently, it is also important to surround yourself with positive people for your work.

Those closest to me cheer me on and also provide tough love. My son, Clayton Tower, inspires me through his work ethic and commitment to family. My mother, Janet, is a selfless, ray of light always striving for kindness and compassion. My soul best friend, Chris Harris, is the constant wind beneath my wings. Without their daily words of encouragement and reminders to "figure it out, Rachel," I am not sure my *Audible* project dreams would have been achieved.

Who collaborated with me?

Audible narrations and productions in romance with Jessica Roe, Lynn Rhys, and Tim Grossi.

The Absolute Intimacy Inventory workbooks are sets of questions for individuals and couples to increase authentic communication. Licensed Clinical Social Worker, Karmaria Negron, and close friend developed these resources with me.

My writing and publishing muses are Darnell Dunn, Jane Baker Smith, and Gail Norwood.

Independently created books, so far, *Third of Eleven, Narrating In My Birthday Suit,* and *Overcoming My Audible Frost.*

What about the foundational pieces mentioned in earlier chapters?

These two works serve as figurative bookends for the early memories and present day.

My profile poem for *ACX* was written for Cathy Edwards as she retired as an English teacher from George Washington High School in Danville, VA. My aunt Cathy was the type of educator I always hoped to be…creative, insightful, and completely devoted to her students. Cancer claimed her shortly after her retirement. I kept the framed poem celebrating educators with me as a reminder to embrace each day. Discovering my voice and love of narration via this piece, simply brings me joy.

For Cathy, On Her Retirement

Thirty years ago a teaching career you began,
But time has now come to say good-bye to friends.

Friends at school and friends in books
Friends who're real, those who're narrative hooks.
So many characters, stories you'll teach no more...
Silas, Antigone, Julius, Shylock, or Portia;
No more Dr. Jekyll and Mr. Hyde
Jekyll has changed for the very last time.
Duncan will die no more at Macbeth's hand;
Beowulf will not sail for the monster's land.
Hamlet will not haunt the castle battlements,
Nor Arthur joust in the Camelot tournaments.
Subject and verb agreement will no longer confuse
Students for whom studying is a habit they refuse,
And the difference between lie and lay
Will fade with the sunset at close of day.
No one to ask, "Do you want me to fail this class?"
Or ask for, please, just one more bathroom pass.
Arguments and fights you'll no longer defuse,
For you will have paid your educational dues.
No more criticals to grade or exams to make,
No more referrals to the office for you to take.
Thirty years, slow and fast, have come and passed;
Oh happy, happy day, retirement is here at last!

May mornings find you lost in the beauty of your flowers, and evenings find you "dancing with the stars."
Deborah Slayton, Neighbor and Friend

MY FIRST SELF-PUBLISHED book happened in Miss Pace's second grade classroom. She was a first year teacher at Unionville Elementary and wore khaki skirts and panty hose. Her hair was brown, perfectly styled in the larger style of the day, and her smile was beautiful. By the end of that school year, we had published two books, learned all about Mt. St. Helens, a few standardized tests, and side-stepped the urban legend of Bloody Mary sweeping the playground. Miss Pace drank iced cafeteria tea from brown cups and was engaged by the end of the year. I adored her.

Second Grade 1984-1985:

All About School

Written and Illustrated by Rachel Edwards

Reprinted exactly from original text.

What is school like? Is it a bad place or is it a nice place? Well, I'll tell you. School is a nice place. You work with scissors and paper and glue and string and pencils and crayons. You read and write and get homework. And you go to P.E. or Music. And come back to your room and go home on the bus. And on Christmas or Halloween or Easter you have parties. What fun! In kindergarten you sit at little tables and in first grade you sit at brown desks. In second grade you have nice yellow desks that shine. You do spelling and math and write books. After a full day you ride the bus home.

After the weekend, the next day is Monday and you go to school as you always do. And when you get there you walk up the sidewalk to the school. And then you study for a hour.

The Bus

The Morning Ride

The bus may look like a bad place. No, it's not. You walk up three steps and get in a seat. You sit in the seat until school. Then you get in a line with rest of the busses and get off.

The Afternoon Ride

Your teacher lines you up and you go out to the bus. Each bus has a number, like 23, 39, 24, 33, 22, 29. You sit down and wait to get off. When you do you tell the bus driver Good bye.

EPILOGUE

Are you hearing your own story, yet?
Let's take a look back and prepare next stages. By sharing parts of my experience narrating my own books, I hope you decide to produce your own work.

By condensing the chapters into actionable steps or stages based on the questions I ask myself throughout creating an audiobook, a manageable checklist emerges.

Stage One (Introduction, Prologue, and Chapter 1): Should I narrate and produce my own book? Am I committed to doing this? Making the decision to narrate your own book.

Stage Two (Chapters 2,3,4, and 5): Where do I start producing my own *Audible?* Initiating the project and preparing materials, software, and websites.

Stage Three (Chapter 6): How do I use my actual strategies for reading? Setting the rehearsal game plan. Comprehension, application, and completion of narration process.

Stage Four (Chapters 7,8,9): What do I do after narrating all my chapters? What's the production cost for my audiobook? What happens if there's a problem with my submitted audiobook? Reframe, personify, and give character traits to technology and self-publishing life to feel more connected to the practice. Execution and evaluation of an *Audible* production.

What comes next?

The narration and production of an audiobook impacts me in the best possible ways. I find joy in printing my words, experiences, and memories in books for others to share. Combining the durability of a paperback and vitality of audio files meets my production needs. That practice takes me to a happy place between my first stage and present day.

The same farmhouses where I learned to love stories told from my mother's mouth also hosted my earliest reading performances. The concrete front porch stages sometimes held imaginary plays and dance performances at my parents' home. My grandmother's front porch stood as stage and audience with family members offering feedback for some school assignment needing polishing and confidence boost on long Sunday afternoons.

While my audiobook production style is often solitary, the earliest audiences are right with me. Emotionally, who is in your audience of memories?

So where are we traveling next? To our next book projects, of course. With a sense of the self-published and self-narrated process, each project will empower creativity and confidence.

Senses of accomplishment through creating your own personal stage tend to linger. Harnessing the power of spoken word and the popular *Audible* catalog of works is a final step in the dynamic self-publishing world.

As you complete your audiobook and share your stories with others, watch for the interested and curious "lean." "Please tell me more about how you did that! I've always wondered how people get started with *Audible!*" audiences will excitedly admit, whisper, or write. Just because you completed your project at home should not take away from your hard work and impactful voice…you are intentional and savvy. Your next production may follow different narration options. But isn't that part of the excitement of publishing your words yourself? Making your own choices and determining what best fits each literary project?

Continue to believe in yourself and support the independent thinking and decision making of all authors. How writers "publish" should not incur judgement- often, we are writing to meet our own needs and artistic expression. Kindness and respect encourages authentic voices and discourages gate keeping.

Tell us a story out of your mouth

So we can now depart

With words performed and meanings met

For this book, author, audience, and every now and then, we must now say…

The End.

www.ingramcontent.com/pod-product-compliance
Lightning Source LLC
Chambersburg PA
CBHW031506040426
42444CB00007B/1229